CROSSING THE LINE
OF FAITH

Also Available

Becoming a Contagious Christian
9780310210085

Becoming a Contagious Christian Curriculum Kit
9780310257851

Becoming a Contagious Christian Participant's Guide
9780310257875

Becoming a Contagious Christian DVD
9780310257882

Becoming a Contagious Christian CD-ROM
9780310257899

Becoming a Contagious Christian Ebook
9780310278498

Becoming a Contagious Christian Audio
9780310259985

CROSSING THE LINE OF FAITH

ZONDERVAN®

ZONDERVAN.com/
AUTHORTRACKER
follow your favorite authors

Crossing the Line of Faith
Copyright © 2008 by Bill Hybels

Requests for information should be addressed to:

Zondervan, *Grand Rapids, Michigan 49530*

Content adapted from *Becoming a Contagious Christian*, copyright © 1994 by Bill Hybels.

Interior design by Mark Sheeres

Printed in the United States of America

08 09 10 11 12 13 • 15 14 13 12 11 10 9 8 7 6 5 4 3 2 1

CONTENTS

1. People Matter to God   7

2. The Rewards of Contagious Christianity   25

3. A Formula for Impacting Your World   43

4. Investing Your Life in People   57

CHAPTER ONE

PEOPLE MATTER TO GOD

THERE'S NOTHING IN LIFE THAT's as exciting as befriending, loving, and leading wayward people toward faith in Christ. Nothing.

In their heart of hearts, I think all true followers of Christ long to become contagious Christians. Though unsure about how to do so or the risks involved, deep down they sense that there isn't anything as rewarding as opening a person up to God's love and truth.

But though we might like the idea of having a spiritual impact on others, we won't take decisive action unless we first raise our motivation level. And one of the best ways to do that is to get God's perspective on the matter.

Let's begin with two lessons, both from unexpected sources. One is from the realm of science, the other from the world of business. The first describes the way things are; the second prescribes the way things ought to be.

A SURPRISING SOURCE

The Anthropic Principle is creating a lot of controversy these days among intellectuals. "Of course," you say, "the Anthropic Principle. I was just reading about that last night before I went to bed!"

Simply stated, the Anthropic Principle implies that when we look at the world around us, it would *seem*, at least at first blush, that the universe was somehow *designed* to support and nourish human life.

This concept, which is very prevalent in the world of secular science and philosophy, didn't originate with Christian scholars. But the evidence points so overwhelmingly toward this apparent design in the universe that it's virtually undeniable by experts of every religious and nonreligious stripe. This has sent skeptics scurrying to find some sort of natural explanation for this apparently supernatural phenomenon.

Here are a few of the hard facts:

- Raise or lower the universe's rate of expansion by even one part in a million, and it would have ruled out the possibility of life.
- If the average distance between stars were any greater, planets like Earth would not have been formed; any smaller, the planetary orbits necessary for life would not have occurred.
- If the ratio of carbon to oxygen had been slightly different than it is, we would not be here to breathe the air.

- Change the tilt of the Earth's axis slightly in one direction, and we would freeze. Change it the other direction, and we'd burn up.
- Suppose the Earth had been a bit closer or further from the sun, or just a little larger or smaller, or if it rotated at a speed any different from the one we're spinning at right now. Given any of these changes, the resulting temperature variations would be completely fatal.

So the lesson we can draw from the Anthropic Principle is this: *someone* must have gone to a lot of effort to make things just right so that you and I could be here to enjoy life. In short, modern science points to the fact that *we must really matter to God.*

A LESSON FROM BUSINESS

There has been a radical transformation in the business arena during the last twenty years that provides an important lesson for Christians.

Management experts talk about these developments in grandiose terms. For example, in *Thriving on Chaos,* Tom Peters refers to this transformation as a "customer revolution." Ken Blanchard, author of the enormously successful book *The One-Minute Manager,* enthusiastically describes what he calls "the upside-down pyramid." What is this change that they believe has been so critical for all of corporate America?

CROSSING THE LINE OF FAITH

Are you ready for this? Hold on to your Dockers: businesses, if they're going to be successful for the long haul, must pull their attention off of themselves and refocus their energies on their only reason for existence—to serve their customers.

Now, before we chide them for going to great lengths to state the obvious, let's note that this advice is sorely needed. How many times do you feel frustrated when you're trying to get basic service in a repair shop, restaurant, bank, bakery, or department store? The natural tendency for these organizations, both big and small, is to become ingrown. Employees begin burning up their energy on internal problems, petty policy disputes, and staff-related strife. And all too often this happens while the customer stands at the checkout counter patiently waiting to be served.

So along came experts like Peters and Blanchard with a challenge that was simple and profound: we must turn over the corporate pyramid and get back to serving the person "at the top"—and that's the customer, *not* the boss. We must work to develop a "customer obsession."

It's not hard to see that both the problems and the solutions of the business world have close cousins within the Christian community. We can get so easily entangled and ensnared in the internal issues, questions, and personal situations in our churches that it's hard to remember that the primary reason we remain on this planet is to reach the people "out there." Just like commercial organizations need to get their focus off themselves, we as individual Christians and collective churches need to recalibrate our sights on the mission God has given us: reaching spiritually lost people.

So if the lesson from science is that people matter to God, then the lesson from business is *they'd better matter to us, too.* Only as we begin to value those outside our Christian circles will we be truly fulfilled and functioning according to God's purpose for us.

But let's be honest. It's hard to keep our focus. Our tendency is to drift away from genuinely valuing the spiritually confused. We're quick to forget how much they matter to God.

AN EYE-OPENING INTERCHANGE

I was reminded of this recently on an out-of-state trip when I bumped into an old acquaintance. He was a man I knew to be a churchgoer, so to get a conversation going, I said to him, "Well, are you looking forward to Easter Sunday?"

As casually as I had asked the question, he replied, "No, I'm not. As a matter of fact, I never go to church on Easter."

"You're kidding!" I said. "You don't go to church on Easter Sunday? You can get arrested for that!"

Ignoring my attempt at humor, he said with some intensity, "I don't go to church on Easter because I can't stand to see all those 'oncers.' You know, the 'annuals,' all the people who only come around once a year. They get themselves all dressed up to make their appearance, and they mess everything up at my church, especially the parking lot. Who do these people think they're fooling? They're not fooling me and they're certainly not fooling God! This has bothered me so much over the years that I just quit going to church on Easter Sunday. I have no use for 'oncers.'"

Although he didn't say it directly, I thought to myself, "Not only does *he* have no use for these people, I'll bet he's convinced that *God* doesn't have any use for them, either."

And you know, as much as I hate to admit it, it's not uncommon for people like me—and maybe like you—to fall prey to similar value judgments. We all tend to make armchair assessments of who God has use for and who He doesn't. And before we know it, we've reduced our mental list of those God really cares about to our own little group of select people who happen to look and act just like us. That list almost never includes the people "out there" who aren't part of the church.

Can you see how dangerous this is? Once we've bought into this line of reasoning, we've imperceptibly but effectively removed any hope of getting motivated to spread God's message of grace. After all, if these people don't matter that much to God, why should we get all worked up about trying to reach them?

AN AGE-OLD ISSUE

This kind of thinking is not new among God's people. We see the same attitudes surfacing in various places throughout the Bible. In fact, one of the central thrusts of Jesus' ministry was to address this issue and challenge his would-be followers to change their view of those outside the family of God.

One day while Jesus was teaching in a sizeable metropolitan area, he found himself surrounded by a large crowd of irreligious people. Oncers. Undesirables. The unconvinced. The spiritually confused. The morally bankrupt people of the town. People God wouldn't *possibly* have any use for.

Off to the side was a huddle of religious leaders who were shaking their heads and talking to each other in muffled tones. They were complaining about the fact that Jesus, who claimed to be the Son of the holy God, was hanging out with *those* kinds of people.

Jesus knew exactly what they were thinking. So he moved the whole procession over to where those in the "holy huddle" were standing. Then, in a steady but forceful tone, he began to tell a pointed and powerful series of stories.

LOST AND FOUND

"There was once a man who owned a hundred sheep," he said. "And while he was tending his sheep, one of those woolly little creatures wandered away. So the shepherd left the ninety-nine behind and went out and searched for the one that was lost. And he kept on searching until he finally found it. He tenderly picked up the sheep, put it around his shoulders, and carried it back to the flock. Then he called some of his shepherd friends and said, 'Let's have a party. I found my wandering sheep!'"

Jesus paused for a moment. Everyone was still listening. "Then there was a woman who had ten coins," he continued. "She lost one of them. So she lit a lamp, swept the house, turned over all the furniture, and searched relentlessly until she found it. And when she did, this woman was so happy that she called her friends and asked them to celebrate with her."

Jesus stopped again and looked around. Maybe he wondered if they were still with him. Then he went on, "There was a man who had two boys, and the younger one got a little cocky. He got stars in his eyes and wanderlust in his heart. He wanted to taste life on the wild side.

"He talked his father into giving him his inheritance early, and he headed out into a distant land with his pockets full of cash. He found the fast lane and the fast crowd and he did some fast living. But he soon found out that the kind of friends he'd found don't stick around long when the money runs out.

"One day while he was feeding pigs to try to support himself, this disoriented, bankrupt boy finally came to his senses. He decided to go back home. He figured he would apologize to his father for his naiveté and immaturity, and then he'd offer to become one of his father's hired hands, since he knew he had forfeited his right to be regarded as his son.

"So he started off for home. His father, who had spent hours each day watching and longing for his son's return, saw him when he was still a long way from the gate. Immediately, the hope-filled father ran down the road to embrace his son. The boy started to say, 'I made an awful mistake, Dad, and I don't deserve to be your son —' But the father interrupted. 'Shhhh, don't talk like that!' he said. 'I'm so glad you're finally home!' He rejoiced and ordered a huge party. He said, 'Invite everyone, kill the fattened calf, and bring out a fresh suit of clothes. My wayward son has come home!' And did they ever have a party!"

Then I think Jesus gazed into the eyes of his listeners and thought, "There — three stories. That ought to make an impression."

You see, this is the only recorded time Jesus ever told three parables in a row. Generally, he would perceive some misunderstanding in the minds of people, size it up, and tell a story that would clarify the issue. Then he'd go on until he saw the next area that needed attention.

But not this time. This particular day Jesus was so upset over the discussion the religious leaders were having about who matters to God and who doesn't, that he said, in effect, "I'm going to clear this up once and for all. I never want there to be confusion on this again. I'm going to tell you not one, not two, but three stories, rapid fire, to make sure everybody understands who really matters to God."

ESSENTIAL ELEMENTS

There are some common threads that run through these stories in Luke 15. The first is that in each one, *something of great value was missing*, something that really mattered. The missing sheep was very important to the shepherd. It represented a significant part of his livelihood. The lost coin was vital to the woman's survival. Quite possibly she was a widow, and what was at stake was a tenth of her entire estate. And, of course, the wayward son mattered greatly to his father.

As Jesus' listeners reflected on these stories, I think some of them began to grasp what he was driving at. It must have taken their breath away when the light finally went on in their heads. This is true especially of the religious leaders whose self-righteous attitudes prompted these stories in the first place.

The more sensitive people in the crowd likely started to think, "Wait! Could it be? Here we are looking down our noses because Jesus is hanging out with these fast-lane irreligious types we thought God had no use for. But Jesus is showing us through these three simple stories that these people — the wanderers, the lost, the spiritually confused — *actually do have value to the heavenly Father*."

When Jesus' listeners put all that together, they were probably crushed by the weight of God's love. A love so large that it could look beyond sins and treasure the wayward people committing them. A love so powerful that it would patiently endure years of resistance, selfish pleasure-seeking, money-chasing, and power-wielding. In the face of all this, God's love says, "Even though you're way off the track, you *still* matter to Me. You really do!"

CONVERSATIONS ON THE CROSS

At the end of Jesus' earthly ministry, the Bible tells us that Jesus was crucified between two thieves. It's important to remember that these guys were serious criminals. They didn't crucify people in those days for petty misdemeanors. These thieves had done some heavy-duty damage, and society had decided it had no further use for them.

While they were hanging on crosses, one of them launched into a verbal tirade. He railed against Jesus, saying that if he was really the Son of God, he should come down from the cross and, while he's at it, take them down, too. The other thief, however, opened his eyes to what was really happening. He realized that in just a short time he would face eternity, and he was painfully aware of the kind of life he had lived.

So, finally, in so many words he blurted out to the other thief, "Shut up! Can't you see what's going on here? Just keep quiet." Then he turned to Jesus and said, "We're getting exactly what we deserve. But you haven't done anything wrong. Furthermore, you know all about me and my life. So excuse me if this is a silly question, but could somebody like me, who has committed all the sins I've committed, still matter to *anybody*?"

What did Jesus say? Without hesitation, he assured this man, "You matter far more than you can imagine! And because of your faith and your tender, repentant spirit, you'll meet up with me just a little later today in Paradise, where we'll be together for all of eternity!"

It's difficult to comprehend compassion like that, isn't it? Let's face it: it's so unlike your love or mine.

A FRIEND IN PAIN

Some time ago, I was studying this passage in Luke 15 and really trying to come to grips with its implications for my life. I was doing my workouts at a health club that had just hired a recent immigrant from India. He was a short, bald guy who spoke broken English and was a little quirky. On top of that, he was a devout Muslim. In other words, he wasn't the kind of person I'd have envisioned as a regular racquetball partner.

But over time I noticed that a lot of the guys at the club didn't want anything to do with this man. Their actions made it clear that he was, to them, a nobody.

There I was, seeing this and trying to grapple with what it means when Jesus says *all* people matter to him. I knew what it meant *theologically.* That part was easy enough. But what did it mean *practically*?

As you might guess, I had to conclude that if everybody matters to God, then this Indian Muslim mattered to him, too.

I started, rather awkwardly at first, to make efforts to befriend him. We talked, we kidded around, we gradually built some rapport. Finally one afternoon I gave him a Bible. To my surprise, the next time I saw him he gave me a copy of the Koran. Turnabout is fair play, I guess.

One day I went to the club after I had been away on a speaking trip. As I was getting dressed to go running, this man came up to me with an anxious look on his face. He said, "Mr. Bill, while you were gone something terrible happened. My wife left me, and now I'm all alone. I just don't know what I'm going to do!"

While he was talking, I remembered that he had a small child. It was easy to see the pain he was in, and I think I was the first person he had talked to about this.

As he went on explaining what had happened, I looked into his eyes, and I sensed that the Holy Spirit was leading me to reach out and embrace this man. Being the ever-obedient spiritual heavy weight that I am, I did what any serious-minded, devoted follower of Christ would do. I called one of those internal time-outs and said to the Lord, "Hold on a minute! Let's not get carried away!"

I told God I had two basic problems with this leading. The first was that I'm not a naturally affectionate person, particularly with men. I'm standing there in the middle of the locker room in my boxer shorts, God's telling me to hug this guy, and I'm thinking, "*How* much does this man matter, God?"

My second problem had to do with this man's religious orientation. I said, "You are aware, Lord, that this fellow you want me to hug is more than merely a non-worshiper. He is actively worshiping the *competition!*"

As you could have predicted, I didn't get very far in reversing the counsel of the eternal, wise, all-knowing King of the universe. Instead, I felt as though the Spirit was saying, "I know all about it, Bill. But I want this man to know in the middle of his pain that he matters to the true God. I'm just looking for one of my children to communicate that to him. Will you do it for me?"

I've got to tell you, it was not an easy step for me. But when I put my arms around the guy, he broke down and flooded my shoulder with his tears. It was clearly an important moment for him. And, in retrospect, it was important to me, too.

A VALUABLE LESSON

Do you see what happened? When I realized how much God cared about this man, it made me care more about him, too. Later on, I admitted to myself how often I, a Christian and a pastor, had done the same ugly, unthinkable things the Pharisees had done. I realized that sometimes I carry around little unpublished lists of people who I don't think are very important. You know, the mechanic who services my car, the waitress, the bell-hop, the cashier, the guy driving the slow-moving car in front of me, the neighbor with the barking dog, the obnoxious intoxicated person sitting next to me on a flight to Los Angeles, the guy at work who doesn't view the world the way I do. These people don't matter very much, right?

The truth is, they *do*. They're important to God. Regardless of race, salary, gender, level of education, religious label or lack thereof, they still matter to him and, therefore, they'd better matter — *really* matter — to me.

When you start to look at others with that kind of attitude, it has a revolutionary effect on the way you treat people. Jesus' stories in Luke 15 tell us that *you have never locked eyes with another human being who isn't valuable to God.* When this fact grips you to the core of your being, you'll never be the same. You will live in awe of the scope and depth and breadth of God's love, and you'll treat people differently.

WE'RE ON A MISSION

Deep in every Christian, there is an awareness that we are on this planet for purposes greater than having a career, paying the bills, loving our families, and fulfilling our role as upstanding citizens. Even going to church and worshiping God — important as these are — sometimes leave us feeling that something is missing. After all, we'll worship God for eternity in heaven; we don't have to be here to do that.

What is it that's absent in the lives of so many believers who are crying out for fulfillment? What on earth is God asking us to do?

God wants us to become contagious Christians — his agents, who will first catch his love and then urgently and infectiously offer it to all who are willing to consider it. This is his primary plan, the one Jesus modeled so powerfully, to spread God's grace and truth person to person until there's an epidemic of changed lives around the world.

This effort is clearly beneficial for people who need

to be reached, but it seems that all the perks flow *their* way. So a natural question is, "What's in it for *me*?"

That's a legitimate question, and it's the focus of our next chapter, "The Rewards of Contagious Christianity." I think you'll be relieved and excited when you discover the multiple benefits for everyone involved. Spreading our faith to other people is genuinely a win-win proposition.

Perhaps a preview will help illustrate how this is true. In fact, it flows right out of the Luke passage we've been looking at, the final common thread in Jesus' three stories: *retrievals result in rejoicing.*

PARTIES IN HEAVEN

The shepherd retrieved the sheep and threw a party. The woman found the coin and threw another party. The son came home and the father threw the biggest party of all. And in Luke 15:10 Jesus says, "In the same way, I tell you, there is rejoicing in the presence of the angels of God over *one sinner* who repents."

When I read that text for the first time, I thought of my own life. I was a cocky, rebellious, self-willed seventeen-year-old who thought I knew how to get to heaven by impressing God with my religiosity. But then, through the influence of the Bible and caring Christian friends, it became clear to me that I could never string together enough righteousness to impress a holy God. What I needed was to admit my sins, turn away from them, and trust Christ to be my forgiver, friend, and leader.

People Matter to God

I remember exactly where I was standing when I took that critical step. I was at a Christian camp in southern Wisconsin, and I just broke down and repented. According to Luke 15:10, do you know what happened next? All of heaven erupted in a magnificent cosmic celebration. There was an enormous party with the honoree's name on the banner—and it was mine! When that dawned on me I remember thinking, "I must *really* matter to God!" It was almost overwhelming to me.

If you're a Christ-follower, the same thing happened when you acknowledged your sin and trusted in him. Whether last week or forty years ago, all of heaven erupted in a party, and *your* name was on the banner. Do you see how much you are treasured by God?

If you think you know what joy is now, just wait until you're a primary player in the process that leads one of your friends to Christ. You're going to almost *explode* with joy when you take part in that person's celestial celebration. That's only natural, especially when you realize that you actually helped get their name on the banner.

There's nothing like the adventure of being used by God to contagiously spread his love, truth, and life to other people—people who matter deeply to him. So let's get on with it!

CHAPTER TWO

THE REWARDS OF CONTAGIOUS CHRISTIANITY

HAVE YOU EVER GOTTEN FIRED up about an idea only to find your enthusiasm fading when you realized the effort it would take to turn the idea into reality?

What about putting away part of your income for retirement or for your child's college education? It's pretty easy to make noble-sounding decisions about appropriate percentages *prior* to actually sitting down with your checkbook. But when you have to make a mortgage payment that takes a third of your income, all of a sudden you're faced with realities that can rob you of your lofty ideals.

Or what about the reconciliation of broken relationships? The best thing to do is to apologize and make amends. After all, that's the path toward renewing friendships. But as good as that sounds, second thoughts often seize us about the time we reach out to pick up the phone or knock on the door.

I could give other examples, but the point is clear: The goal may be noble, the intentions sincere, and the plan in place. But we can still end up not taking action. What holds us back at the point of following through?

Often what's lacking is a clearheaded and open-eyed examination of the real costs and rewards. Without this, the plan can *sound* good but lack the personal *pull* required to transform ideas into action. You must be convinced that having funds laid aside for later or enjoying a restored relationship is worth the effort and expense.

WEIGHING THE OPTIONS

Business managers understand this and have developed something called a cost/benefit analysis to help them see the whole picture. This is a tool designed to give them a realistic projection of what the proposed course of activity will require on the investment side, as well as what it will yield on the payback side. Armed with that information, they can then make informed decisions and stick to them with minimal surprises along the way.

Each of us does something similar when making a tough choice about which way to turn. Whether it's on paper or just in our minds, we put all the pros on one side of the ledger and the cons on the other. This informal analysis helps us choose the course that makes the most sense.

Jesus suggested a similar approach in Luke 14, where he used two illustrations, one involving constructing a building and the other, going to war. The lesson in both cases was the same: before embarking on a project, add up what you'll have to invest—"count the cost"—to make sure it's worth the effort and that you'll be able to follow it through to completion.

Now let's relate this to becoming contagious Christians. We've already established that people matter to God and ought to matter to us. We also know that apart from Christ they're lost, and that their inherent worth as humans warrants an all-out search. But has anybody bothered to check lately to see how much these all-out searches cost? The price on the tag doesn't seem to be the bargain it might once have been!

The truth is, it never was. While reaching out to irreligious people may sound good on the surface, you don't have to look very deeply before you realize the actual rescue effort is going to entail significant personal expense. And if that's true for one lost person, just imagine the combined tab when we start trying to reach whole families, communities, and countries!

Before we get all feverish about the concept of contagious Christianity, maybe we ought to slow down and do our own cost/benefit analysis in order to project how this enterprise will come out.

First, let's reverse the order. We'll start with the benefits and then spell out some costs. Next, we'll weigh the two sides and decide where we should go from there. If the price is too high, you can cash in this book for the latest John Grisham novel. But if it goes the other way, we'll roll up our sleeves and get busy. Fair enough?

PERSONAL BENEFITS OF CONTAGIOUS CHRISTIANITY
Adventure

You've probably thought of communicating your faith as an important obligation, something you may feel guilty about not doing more. But until you really dive in, you won't realize that extending Christ to others can give your relationship with him an exciting sense of the unexpected.

God gets great pleasure from sending his agents on secret reconnaissance missions with personal instructions no one else knows about. He loves to stretch us beyond our comfort zones and challenge us to take risks on the front lines of his kingdom-advancement enterprises. He delights in giving us action-on-the-edge where, with white knuckles, we'll cling to him as he takes us on the spiritual ride of our lives. The thrilling part is that he does this to help us grow as well as to spread his love to more and more wayward people.

In other words, the Christian life is one of faith, where we find ourselves routinely overdriving our headlights but knowing it's okay because God is in control and has a purpose behind it.

Does this image excite you? If not, it might be a sign that you've been playing it safe in your spiritual life. Maybe it's time to take steps toward becoming a more contagious Christian, one God can use in his exciting search-and-rescue mission.

I know what it's like to have my spiritual life get

stagnant, and then to see God open an opportunity to speak for him. I rarely feel completely prepared, but it's always exhilarating when I open my mouth anyway and begin to sense that he's using me.

My trip to the health club was looking like just another mundane fifty-five minutes of laps and reps until my Indian Muslim friend walked up and poured his heart out to me. Suddenly I knew God had transformed an ordinary workout into an extraordinary faith-adventure.

A friend of mine was having a muffler put on his car not long ago. Sitting in the customer waiting room was hardly the highlight of his week, but he decided to make the most of the time by looking over his workbook from our church's evangelism seminar that he'd recently completed.

"What's that you're reading?" a stranger suddenly asked. And just that fast, Dave's visit to Midas was transformed from a nuisance into a golden opportunity.

It was just another of numerous weekly flights for a commercial pilot who attends Willow Creek Community Church. There wasn't anything special about the night or unusual about the weather on this routine trip from O'Hare to L.A.

Nothing out of the ordinary—until he struck up a spiritual conversation with his copilot and, at 4:30 A.M. in the cockpit of a 727 at 28,000 feet, ended up leading him in a prayer of commitment to Christ. Now, *that's* adventure.

Is your spiritual life lacking some action? Do you want to see God turn the routine into the remarkable? God is waiting to make it happen, and that's just one of the benefits of becoming a contagious Christian.

Purpose

As you begin to experience more and more of the adventures God can create out of everyday situations, you'll find yourself facing daily tasks with a whole new sense of purpose. You'll start anticipating that he might surprise you at any time with an eternity-altering opportunity.

Trips to the health club, muffler shop, or your workplace become, in your mind, thinly veiled excursions into the realm of divine possibility. You'll start asking yourself, "Just what might God be up to in *this* situation?"

Part of the excitement of this perspective is that you may begin to see the hand of God even behind difficult events and circumstances.

Some time ago our church published its own magazine. In order to capture a story about a hospital we were helping, we sent our editor and our photographer to Haiti. Their week went according to plan—until they got to the airport and boarded their home-bound six-seat chartered airplane.

Suddenly two soldiers who had been part of a failed coup attempt jumped the airport's security fence and stormed the small aircraft with machine guns and explosives in hand. As they forced their way aboard the plane, they demanded in broken English to be flown immediately to Miami.

It was a dangerous situation that could have ended in disaster. But my colleagues were able to view their predicament as something with divine purpose.

After their plane had taken off, they managed to ease tensions by asking the two soldiers about their families. Before they knew it, the weapons had been put away and they were sharing cans of Coke with them as they continued to talk and even laugh together. And if that isn't amazing enough, before the flight was over they had drawn a gospel illustration on a piece of paper in an effort to explain God's love and the forgiveness he offers through Christ.

It didn't make much difference who these soldiers were or what they had done. They still mattered to God, and they needed to know it. It was that awareness that put *purpose* into what was otherwise a difficult and dangerous situation.

It's incredible to realize that what we do each day has meaning in the big picture of God's plan.

Fulfillment

As we begin to throw ourselves into rescuing irreligious people and looking for purpose in everyday events, we start to feel a sense of fulfillment that transcends the realm of everyday human experience. What else could compare to being an instrument in God's hand, used to communicate his love and clarify his truth to people he cared enough to die for? There's nothing more satisfying than effectively furthering God's redemptive purpose for humanity.

Recently, Mark, the coauthor of this book, attempted to communicate Christ to a fifty-seven-year-old Jewish man. You can imagine the time and energy he spent talking with a man who had been steeped in the Jewish faith and culture for so many years. But when Mark finally prayed with this man to embrace Jesus as his Messiah, you'd better believe he felt some major-league fulfillment. And when they met a year later to celebrate the one-year spiritual birthday of this man, who was now attending a seminary to prepare for full-time ministry, Mark could barely contain the joy he felt.

Spiritual Growth

When lethargic believers break out of spiritual isolation and interact with spiritual seekers, something incredible starts to happen. As they experience the high-stakes conversations that tend to happen with unchurched people, they begin to notice a sort of inner renewal taking place. Areas long ignored suddenly come alive with fresh significance.

Scripture reading, for example, becomes revitalized. They used to pull out the Bible once in a while, partly to see what they could learn from it and partly to alleviate some guilt. But now they've *got* to read it—even *memorize* parts of it—in order to know what they're talking about in the next exchange of spiritual ideas.

What's really exciting is that in addition to gearing up for talking with others, they start to renew a genuine desire for fresh glimpses into God's character and truth. So what started as dutifully helping someone else changes into a personal desire for intimacy with God.

Similar changes happen in the area of prayer. Talking to God suddenly takes on new purpose. Stale recitations get displaced by impassioned pleas for the salvation of destruction-bound friends. And as spiritual progress is noticed in their lives, enthusiasm for prayer escalates all the more because there are now fresh reasons to thank him, as well as critical concerns to bring his way.

The benefits don't stop there. As we all know, the hardest part of prayer is getting started. But concern for our spiritually confused friends can jump-start us, and our conversations with God will spill over into all kinds of diverse areas. We find ourselves once again experiencing living and growing prayer lives.

Our desire to worship God grows, too. How could you *not* express gratitude to a God who so graciously and patiently extends his love to rebels like we were and like many of our friends still are? Naturally you start praising God for who he is and what he does, and before you know it you find you've again become a sincere worshiper.

What about personal purity? A benefit of becoming a contagious Christian is that it helps you maintain a high standard of conduct. You gain a heightened awareness that you're God's representative and that what you do really matters because it positively or negatively impacts the lives of others.

I know a man at our church who couldn't kick the habit of excessive gambling at the local race track. After many frustrating rounds of quitting and starting again, he had reluctantly decided to just live with it. But then one of our staff members challenged him on it: not because it's the ultimate sin, but because it was hindering his ability to influence his friends for Christ.

With newfound motivation, this man gave up "playing the ponies" once and for all. Interestingly, he is now one of the most contagious Christians in our church.

There's another important aspect to this area of personal purity: when you start going on record with those around you that you're a serious Christian, they begin immediately and instinctively to watch your life. Some do it out of curiosity, others out of a desire to find fault. Either way, it provides a highly effective system of accountability. Your irreligious friends actually assist you in becoming a more godly man or woman, which is an added bonus to our list of personal benefits.

The last item on our spiritual growth list is church involvement. Having a heightened sense of concern for lost people will affect our participation in two ways. First, it will motivate us to take advantage of all that our church offers to help us grow in spiritual strength and stamina. Second, it will provoke us to make changes in our churches in areas that may have become outdated, inefficient, or even counterproductive. We begin to realize that the task of the church is too important to let it run on fewer than eight cylinders. So with fresh motivation, we start helping the church become all it was meant to be in order to reach irreligious people and turn them into fully devoted followers of Christ.

Isn't it incredible how elevating our efforts to reach others can be a catalyst for personal growth? But in case that's not enough, here are a few other benefits.

Spiritual Confidence

Engaging in efforts to extend your faith to others can go a long way toward strengthening your confidence in your own beliefs. This is true, in part, because talking to people who have different spiritual perspectives will force you to take steps to ensure you are speaking accurately about the Christian faith.

We automatically increase our own knowledge when we try to communicate our faith to friends who are skeptics, or Mormons, or Jehovah's Witnesses, or New Agers, or even church-going non-Christians. And when we successfully hold our own in the face of opposition, we gain a heightened sense of spiritual confidence.

And if you think that builds your self-assurance, imagine what happens when one of these people becomes a Christian. Your faith is boosted sky high. You may feel like seeking out some Muslim fundamentalists or hardened atheists. Why not? They matter to God, too. Truly, there's no telling who he'll use you to reach, once your spiritual confidence starts spiraling upward.

The Honor of Being God's Agent

When we realize how great God is and how weak and dependent we are, the words of Jesus in Acts 1:8 become almost incomprehensible: "You will receive power when the Holy Spirit comes on you; and you will be my witnesses in Jerusalem, and in all Judea and Samaria, and to the ends of the earth."

Can't you see the disciples turning and looking behind themselves to see who he was talking to? I can imagine them saying, "Who, *us*? Lord, you've *got* to be kidding! We were just getting used to the fact that you came back to life, and now you're going to take off and leave this whole kingdom-expansion project to *us*? This is *incredible*!"

And it's no less amazing — or true — today than it was then. Hard as it is to grasp, God has chosen us to be his agents. He's given us the high honor of speaking on his behalf. And he promises to empower and use us in the process.

I'll never forget one of the first times this really hit home for me. It was during my early ministry days when I was working with high school students. We had planned a big Wednesday night outreach event, and all of our members worked hard to invite their friends to hear the gospel message, perhaps for the first time.

The night came, the place was full, and it was almost time for me to step onto the stage. I remember feeling an extreme case of "the ordinaries." Maybe this happens to you, too. You start thinking things like, "Who am *I* to be getting up there talking to all these kids? I barely know this stuff myself, so what makes me think I can convey anything meaningful to them?"

Even now, after many years of ministry, I often get hit with a wave of the ordinaries. But it helps me to remember that it was *God* who bestowed upon us the high honor of being his representatives. It wasn't our idea. So while we need to pray and prepare, in a very real sense what happens from there is his problem. And as I found out that night so long ago, it's a problem he loves to solve in order to show his power by doing the extraordinary through us.

In spite of my self-doubt, and knees that were literally shaking, I got up and explained to these students to the best of my limited abilities that they mattered to God. And I told them it wasn't enough for them to believe God loved them, but that they also needed to come to Christ to receive his forgiveness and leadership. And when I asked them to take that step, I was amazed to see several hundred students stand to their feet.

In fact, I was so startled that I thought they'd misunderstood me. So I told them to sit back down so I could re-explain the gospel and the kind of commitment I was talking about. And then, even *more* of them stood to their feet.

Beyond my wildest dreams, God had honored the feeble efforts of one of his apprentice ambassadors as he altered the eternities of scores of high school students. I remember afterward walking behind the building we had met in, leaning against a wall, and being over-whelmed with feelings of gratitude and amazement that he would use someone like me.

And guess what? He can use someone like *you,* too. It might not be in front of high school students, but perhaps over a fence, at a desk, at a table in a restaurant, at a construction site, on a basketball court, or on a podium. God has bestowed on you the honor of being his spokesperson. He has promised that he'll honor your efforts to become a contagious Christian by rewarding you and touching others.

Are those enough personal benefits to whet your appetite? We haven't even talked about all that the recipients of our efforts will gain. You know, little stuff, like escaping the prospect of hell and gaining the promise of heaven, not to mention having a life here on earth filled with adventure, purpose, fulfillment, growth, spiritual confidence, lasting investments, and the honor of becoming agents for the God of the universe.

On top of that, God benefits when you're a contagious Christian, too. He has the reward of watching his children emulate his love for lost people, a kind of joy any parent can readily understand. John 15:8 says, "This is to my Father's glory, that you bear much fruit. . . ." In addition, remember that when we are successful in leading someone to faith, Luke 15:10 tells us that "there is rejoicing in the presence of the angels of God over one sinner who repents." It's a celestial celebration.

But one question remains. Just what is the cost of this kind of personal outreach, and does it offset our extensive list of benefits?

THE COSTS OF CONTAGIOUS CHRISTIANITY
Time and Energy

You know and I know that reaching wayward people will not be easy. It will involve the expending of time and energy, our most valued resources, in order to build relationships, showing Christian care and compassion, and praying consistently. It will involve explaining and re-explaining the seemingly simple gospel message, waiting patiently while they "think about it" (knowing that in many cases they're really running from it), trying to cope with myriad challenging questions, and, in the back of your mind, realizing that they might end up rejecting Christ. It sounds like a formula for frustration, doesn't it?

But let me ask this: How better could you expend your time and energy than investing it in people, many of whom will thank you for all of eternity in heaven? What other investment will reap so high a reward?

Reading and Study

In order to reach others, it's going to take some Bible study and, occasionally, reading books like this one. But is this really so bad? Sure, it takes some effort to make certain you know what you're talking about, but you'd want to be up on what you believe anyway, wouldn't you? Scripture tells all of us to keep growing in our knowledge and understanding of God. Besides, it's not fair to list Bible study on the cost side of the equation when we've already listed it on the benefit side.

Money

It's true that investing in the lives of others takes a tangible investment. Lunches, cell-phone minutes, the cost of books, conferences, and the sometimes high expense of providing for the physical needs of others — these are some of the financial demands contagious Christianity can have on our wallets.

But when the tab is totaled, the amount of hard cash spent is usually still relatively low, especially in comparison to the overwhelming rewards that result. And for those situations where the cost is higher, these words of Jesus offer appropriate encouragement: "Store up for yourselves treasures in heaven, where moth and rust do not destroy, and where thieves do not break in and steal. For where your treasure is, there your heart will be also" (Matt. 6:20–21). I can't imagine a safer investment, can you?

Risk of Embarrassment, Rejection, or Persecution

While probably few of us suffer overt persecution, the likelihood is high that we'll experience some lesser kinds of resistance. It could be teasing from friends or just the lonely feeling of being left out of certain conversations or social gatherings. But it can also get more serious when there's discrimination or intentional harassment because of what we represent.

I don't have any easy answers. I would only encourage you to ask God for his vantage point as you look at the benefits of obeying him. He offers comfort through verses like, "Blessed are you when people insult you, persecute you and falsely say all kinds of evil against you because of me. Rejoice and be glad, because great is your reward in heaven" (Matt. 5:11 – 12), and "Let us not become weary in doing good, for at the proper time we will reap a harvest if we do not give up" (Gal. 6:9).

It Complicates Your Life

For most of us, the primary cost of reaching others is that it entangles us in the concerns and activities of their lives. It encroaches upon our independence. It adds details to our overloaded schedules. Simply stated, it complicates our already complicated lives.

But so does getting married. And having children. And buying a house. And, for that matter, becoming a Christian. Think about it. All of these areas require time, effort, learning, some risk, and, without question, a fair share of money. Most of the things that are important complicate our lives. But are they worth it? Of course they are!

THE OUTCOME

Sure, there are costs, efforts, risks, and complications involved, but when you become a contagious Christian it's worth it — a thousandfold. The closer you look, the more you see that the rewards are high and the costs relatively low, especially when we understand that ultimately they're not costs at all. *They're investments that pay permanent dividends.*

When I see the way the scales tip decisively in our cost/benefit analysis, it fires me up to get on with the adventure at hand: namely, considering how can we take steps toward heightening our contagiousness and begin to experience all the rewards God has for us. That's the subject we'll explore in the next chapter.

CHAPTER THREE

A FORMULA FOR IMPACTING YOUR WORLD

ONE OF THE MOST FRUSTRATING experiences in life is to be told what to do without being given a clear idea of how to go about doing it. Unfortunately, this kind of thing happens all the time.

Your boss sets a sky-high sales quota and lets you know in no uncertain terms that he expects you to meet it. He informs you that overall revenue must be raised, costs lowered, and the bottom line improved, but how you get it all done is *your* problem.

Or your teacher barks out more and more assignments as the books and homework pile up, and the frustration grows. Read this, write that, work it out, turn it in, take the exam, pass the course. And the professor seems unconcerned that you have four other classes with equally high demands. You'll just have to work it out somehow, but how you do it is a test you'll have to take alone. No wonder so many of have frequent nightmares about uncompleted classes.

Even in church we're bombarded with expectations to have strong marriages, obedient children, God-honoring budgets, ethical businesses, effective prayer lives, and meaningful relationships. But while the "ought to" comes through loudly and clearly, the "how to" often remains distant and muffled, if it's heard at all.

One place where this is especially true is in the challenge to have an evangelistic impact on your world. "People are lost," the preacher exclaims. "They're headed for hell, God wants to reach them, and you're his chosen ambassador — so you'd better get out there and bring them to Christ!"

How can you argue with that? It's biblical, it rings true, and it makes sense. So here I go to take some action on it — but where? Could somebody elaborate on that technical term "get out there"? How do I get started? What does the process look like? Who will help me take the first step?

A DIVINE PLAN

Thank God he didn't leave us in such a state of confusion. There's an old saying, "What God expects, he enables." Not only does he tell us that this world of wayward people matters to him, but he also sees to it that we have the information we need to start us on the path of effectively reaching them.

Jesus talked about his plan for doing this a long time ago when he sat with his followers on the side of a hill near Capernaum. Using everyday terms, he explained principles that can be boiled down to this precise plan for influencing our world:

A Formula for Impacting Your World

$$HP + CP + CC = MI$$

What does this cryptic equation mean? While it may look like something out of a chemistry textbook, it's actually a formula that contains God's strategy for reaching spiritually lost people.

We'll break with standard algebra and start right off with the last element, MI. That means *Maximum Impact:* to have the greatest spiritual influence possible on those around us. This is God's purpose, expressed throughout the Bible.

As we've seen, Acts 1:8 tells us we are to be his witnesses, empowered by his Spirit to reach people near and far. Second Corinthians 5:19 says that when we've been reconciled with God through Christ, we are given the ministry of helping sinful men and women come to peace with God. Matthew 28:19–20, often referred to as the Great Commission, tells us to go into the whole world, spread the gospel message, lead people to Christ, and then baptize and build them up in the faith. Elsewhere Jesus says we are to be fishers of men.

Scripture is brimming with challenges to each of us to arrange our lives so that we can have the highest possible spiritual influence on those around us. It's our responsibility to put those challenges into action; it's his to produce results by drawing people to himself.

Before we explore the rest of our formula's component parts, we need to examine its source. It flows out of two elements Jesus used as illustrations: salt and light.

It was in the middle of the greatest sermon in history, the Sermon on the Mount, that Jesus said these famous words: "You are the salt of the earth . . . you are the light of the world." He wanted all of his followers to see themselves as salt and light in how they lived out their lives in the world.

A NEW VIEW OF SALT

Let's look at the first one. Why would Jesus use a metaphor like salt? What does salt do? These days, it makes us nervous because it can lead to high blood pressure. We feel guilty every time we reach for the shaker. But let's look across the span of time and think about the primary uses of salt throughout history.

The first thing that comes to mind is that salt makes us thirsty. Which, I'm told, is why bars serve salty pretzels and peanuts free of charge, to get people to drink more.

Salt does something else, too: it flavors things up. Who'd want corn on the cob without it? When we eat something that tastes a little bland we reflexively reach for the salt in order to enhance the taste.

And salt preserves. We don't use it for this purpose much anymore, but before the days of the Frigidaire, salt was widely used to prevent foods from spoiling. Certain meats could be preserved for long periods of time if they were carefully packed in salt.

So salt stimulates thirst, it adds excitement to the taste of things, and it holds back decay. Which leads us to the big question: Which of these did Jesus have in mind when he looked at his followers and said, "You are the salt of the earth"?

It could be that Jesus meant for salt to symbolize the idea of creating thirst. When Christians are in tune with the Holy Spirit, and when they live in their world with a sense of purpose, and with peace and joy, this often creates a spiritual thirst in the people around them.

When Christians live out their faith with authenticity and boldness, they put a little zing into a sometimes bland cup of soup. They catch people off guard and make them wince. They wake people up with their challenges and seemingly radical points of view. And they overturn a few applecarts here and there. In short, they put some spice into the lives of those around them.

What's more, when believers are living Christ-honoring lives they hold back the moral decay in society. I hope that's what's happening with the abortion dilemma, with environmental concerns, with racism, and with the breakdown of the family. As Christians honor God, he uses them to stem the tidal wave of evil that's threatening to sweep the land.

So pick a card — any card. Any or all three might be exactly what Jesus had in mind when he used the word "salt." But upon further reflection you might discover additional reasons Jesus chose the salt metaphor, reasons that can be easily overlooked.

First, in order for salt to have the greatest possible impact, it must be potent enough to have an effect.

And second, for any impact to take place, salt has to get close to whatever it's supposed to affect. So Jesus may have chosen the salt metaphor because salt requires both *potency* and *proximity* to do its thing.

That leads us back to the formula:

$$HP + CP + CC = MI$$

Having established that the end purpose of the formula is to produce *Maximum Impact*, we can now move to the front and look at the first two elements needed to reach that goal: HP + CP. HP means *High Potency*, and CP, *Close Proximity*.

That's exactly what we need as Christians if we're going to influence people who are outside the family of God. We must have high potency, which means a strong enough concentration of Christ's influence in our lives that his power and presence will be undeniable to others. And we've got to have plenty of proximity. We need to get close to people we're hoping to reach in order to allow his power to have its intended effect.

In Matthew 5:13 Jesus said that salt that is without savor and of inferior quality is worthless. It has lost its power. It won't create much thirst, won't add much spice, won't retard much decay. It can have all kinds of proximity—it can be poured all over something we want it to affect—but if it lacks potency it is, Jesus said, useless. About all it does is give people something to stomp on.

By the same token, highly flavored, industrial-strength salt has great potency, but it can't produce any results unless it touches something. As author Becky Pippert wrote many years ago, unless salt gets poured out of the shaker, it remains a mere table ornament.

That, unfortunately, is a fairly good description of a lot of people who call themselves Christians. Oh, they've got a lot of potency in their own relationship with Christ. They walk a God-honoring path in their personal patterns of living. But they never get out where they can rub up next to people who need their influence. They're good-looking table ornaments, but they have low impact.

Do you see why Jesus' choice of the salt metaphor was so compelling? With it he was able to show that both components—potency and proximity—have to be employed before we can fulfill our mission to have a spiritual impact on our family and friends.

A POWERFUL EXAMPLE

A few years ago my wife and I spent a day with Billy and Ruth Graham at their mountaintop home in North Carolina. In the evening I could tell Billy was starting to get tired, so I told him we were going to head back to our hotel. But to my surprise he handed me his Bible and said, "Bill, before you go, feed me from God's Word."

I thought to myself, this seasoned leader is obviously *not* a baby Christian. And there's no savor problem here, either. In addition, he has communicated the gospel message to more people than anyone else in history. Yet here he was saying to me, in effect, "I still need and love to be fed from God's Word."

This experience helped me understand why Billy Graham has maintained such a high-potency factor for so long. He continually takes steps to heighten his saltiness. Nothing that happened during our time together lingered with me more than that did. I left, hoping that my savor factor will be sky high when I'm that age. I would like to be *dangerous* when I'm in my later years — wouldn't you?

How is that going to happen? It'll happen when we take the steps that make us highly potent at age eighteen, and thirty-eight, and fifty-eight. What are they? I wish I could offer you a spine-tingling, bungy-jumping kind of answer, but I can't. It comes, rather, by practicing the age-old daily spiritual disciplines that have made believers salty for thousands of years, and there's nothing fancy or high-tech about it.

High potency comes from reading and feeding on the truths of the Bible. It comes from being on our knees in prayer. It comes from rubbing shoulders with other contagious Christians in small group fellowships, where brothers and sisters in Christ attempt to take the masks off and be real with each other. It comes from serving and contributing in a biblically functioning church. It comes from trying to actively share your faith with others, and experiencing both successes and failures along the way. It comes from disciplining ourselves for the purpose of sustained saltiness.

A Formula for Impacting Your World

When it comes to developing and maintaining high potency, there's no magic wand and there are no short-cuts. Our savor factor will be roughly proportionate to the extent to which we engage in the age-old spiritual disciplines. Daily contact with God and his Word will keep us open to the Spirit's leadings, eager to influence people outside the family, loving and tender before God and each other, and tuned into what's really important.

These activities will not only keep us tapped into God's divine power, they will also help us develop the traits of a contagious Christian, which we'll discuss in the next section.

There aren't many Billy Grahams around, but we can all take steps to raise our understanding of what it takes to have high potency. Undoubtedly, each of us has room to grow in character and in connectedness to God so as to become stronger salt. The way you live your life can create thirst, add flavor, and serve as a moral preservative as you interact with those around you.

A LESSON FROM LIGHT

As we saw earlier, salt was just one of two metaphors Jesus used in describing what his followers should be like. The other was light. He said in Matthew 5:14, "You are the light of the world." It is again appropriate to ask what made Jesus choose this metaphor. What does light do?

The most basic answer is that it makes things visible and helps us see them for what they really are. It's what we mean when we say we want to "shed some light" on an issue.

And when we look into the biblical use of the term "light," the central idea that emerges is that of clearly and attractively presenting God's truth to others, *illuminating* it in order to show it for what it really is. And while the metaphor includes the need to model a lifestyle that will stand in contrast to the drabness of life without Christ, the distinctive idea seems to be that of lucidly articulating the content of the gospel message.

This can be seen in other Scripture passages that refer to light. For example, in 2 Corinthians 4:5–6, we're told that when the message of Christ was first clarified to us, God "made his light shine in our hearts to give us *the light of the knowledge of the glory of God* in the face of Christ." Do you see the link between light and the conveying of information about the gospel message?

Similarly, in the Matthew passage, Jesus seems to be saying he wants his followers to be able to spiritually illuminate others not only by living out his teachings, but also by explaining his message of forgiveness and grace with precision and accuracy. That's what it is to be light.

So just as the salt illustration gave us the first two components of our formula, HP (high potency) + CP (close proximity), so now the light metaphor provides the final component of our formula for having maximum impact on others. It is CC, which stands for *Clear Communication* of the gospel message. Putting it all together, we get:

A Formula for Impacting Your World

$$\text{HP} + \text{CP (salt)} + \text{CC (light)} = \text{MI}$$

For light to have its intended effect, Jesus says in Matthew 5:15–16, it must not be covered up or obscured in any way. And in order for us to have the powerful influence God desires, we must know the gospel message cold and be ready to communicate it concisely and clearly.

This implies that we'll have to do some extra work to learn how to declare and defend the major tenets of the gospel with straightforward simplicity. We need to be ready to help people understand God's nature, their sinfulness, Christ's payment, and the step each of us must take to receive the forgiveness and new life he offers.

Far too many Christians have been anesthetized into thinking that if they simply live out their faith in an open and consistent fashion, the people around them will see it, want it, and somehow figure out how to get it for themselves. Or they reason that maybe these people will come and ask them what makes their life so special and, when they do, they'll seize the opportunity and explain it to them. But let's be honest: that almost never happens.

While it's a prerequisite to live a salty Christian life —to be highly potent and in relationship with others— that alone is not enough. God forbid that we stop there, because people end up in hell on that plan. It's imperative that we also put the message into clear language our friends can understand and act upon.

Paul asks in Romans 10:14, "How can they believe in the one of whom they have not heard? And how can they hear without someone preaching to them?" Jesus said we should not only be salt, but also light: clearly communicating His message of grace. If we're both, we'll enable the people we care about to do what He says in Matthew 5:16. After they've had an opportunity to "see your good deeds" and understand the central gospel message, they'll be ready to make a decision to follow Christ and meaningfully "praise your Father in heaven."

MAKING AN HONEST ASSESSMENT

So let's pause to ask the big question: does this equation accurately describe the current condition of your own life? Take a look at it one more time while you think about this important question.

HP/high potency + CP/close proximity + CC/clear communication = MI/maximum impact

I know many people for whom this is an accurate description. I marvel at the degree of savor in their spiritual lives. And I'm thrilled to see the lengths to which they'll go to rub shoulders with irreligious people in order to influence them for Christ. These people inspire and challenge me.

But many other Christians are flirting with funny arithmetic. They're trying to get a sort of "new math" to work. They say, "I'm going to figure out a way to make high potency and *low* proximity add up to maximum impact." But they can't succeed, because they remain isolated from the very people they need to touch.

Others say, "I'll have all the proximity you can imagine. I'll run with those crowds so much that I'll become *indistinguishable*! And then I'll have maximum impact." No you won't—not until you have distinctiveness, potency, and savor.

Many more people try to conclude the matter by saying, "Okay, I'll get my savor factor up high by living a consistent Christian life, and then I'll exert the needed efforts to get into influence-range with the people I'd like to reach. But please don't ask me to actually *say* anything! I'll just live out my faith in front of them and maybe some of it will begin to rub off."

As time will prove, however, that's only wishful thinking. Just as words without actions are futile, actions without words are devoid of meaning and content. Can you see why Jesus emphasized that we need to be both salt *and* light? It's critical that we have a high savor factor *and* a readiness to articulate the message of Christ.

CHAPTER FOUR

INVESTING YOUR LIFE IN PEOPLE

"WE'RE HERE," THE MAN SAID warmly to his wife. "Copacabana Beach, the top floor, a beautiful restaurant, and a first-class hotel. It's been worth it, hasn't it, honey? Working and saving all these years were worth it for a night like tonight."

I couldn't help overhearing this couple at the table next to mine as I sat alone, thinking about all I'd seen over the previous few weeks. I was on the last leg of a month-long trip my father had sent me on throughout Central and South America to deliver money to missionaries he was supporting there. And since I was going that direction, he'd put together an itinerary with stops in several cities throughout South America, just so I could more fully experience that part of the world.

It was a very formative time in my life. I was nineteen years old. I'd recently become a Christian but didn't know yet what I was going to do for the rest of my life. I'd begun the journey with a tribe of native Americans in the middle of the Central American jungle, where a church was flourishing. It was an exciting place. The

Holy Spirit was active, and lives were being changed throughout the whole region.

From there I'd gone through several other cities, and ended up in Rio de Janeiro, Brazil, which at the time was the jet-set capital of the world. And now I was having dinner alone in an elegant restaurant, hearing this couple discuss how wonderful it was to finally be there.

I felt almost dizzy as I thought to myself, "Wait a minute. These people are about sixty years old, and they're saying they've waited a lifetime to experience *this*? I'm nineteen and I'm already sitting here! What am *I* going to do for the next thirty or forty years? If this is *It,* I'm in big trouble. It's nice, but it certainly isn't *It.*"

I remember walking back to my room thinking, "What am I going to do with my life? What's important enough for me to invest my whole future in?"

As I reflected on the years I'd been working in my dad's company, many fond memories flashed through my mind. But I also sensed that it was not a career that would meet the yearning in my spirit to be part of something eternal and transforming.

By comparison, I thought back to that little church in the middle of the jungle, and the number of really sharp people who had given their lives to serve among the natives there. They'd built an amazing community of believers who were now leading their friends to Christ. I remembered sitting on the ground just days earlier during one of their worship services as they sang their hearts out in praise to God.

That night in Rio de Janeiro, I realized that what I'd seen happening in that tribe was more real, more lasting, and more important than just raking in more profits in the business world. And it was something I wanted to be part of.

As it turned out, that was a thought I was never able to shake, in spite of all the allurements and opportunities that would try to pull me in other directions.

THE FISHING BUSINESS

It's an age-old struggle. I wasn't just wrestling with which profession to choose. I was grappling with where to invest my passion, dreams, and energy. I later realized that I was in good company when I read in the New Testament that some of Jesus' disciples wrestled with this issue, too.

Though fishermen by trade, Peter and Andrew had taken seriously Jesus' challenge in the fourth chapter of Matthew, where he had said to them, in effect, "I understand your preoccupation with catching fish. But hear me, friends, and hear me well. If you'll trust me and follow me, if you'll try to understand who I am and what I'm up to in this world, then you'll also let me make you fishers of men. And believe me, this is infinitely more significant an endeavor than merely catching fish!"

It's important to understand that Jesus was not knocking the fishing business, any more than he would have knocked the construction business, from which he and Joseph had made a living. There's nothing wrong with those occupations, or the food business, the travel business, the insurance business, or the real estate business. They're all fine. But no earthly enterprise is as important as the business of bringing lost people to the cross of Christ. This should be central to the lives of all of his followers, regardless what they do for a career.

Those who choose to follow Christ will eventually come to the conclusion that there's nothing more important than reaching people. And when they do, their values will change forever. They'll be seized by the realization that every other earthly activity pales in comparison with helping an individual man, woman, boy, or girl come into a saving, liberating, life-changing relationship with the God of the universe.

And once they understand that the most important business in the world is the people business, watch out! They're going to live differently, pray differently, love differently, work differently, give differently, and serve differently, because they'll be preoccupied with people and their needs. They'll become consumed with how they can be more effective fishers of men.

I was sitting in the sales office of my father's produce company in Michigan when I read a few verses in the third chapter of 2 Peter that described the fiery fate of all the things I had been so concerned about getting.

The thought just overwhelmed me; what a futile waste of effort to invest myself in obtaining so much temporal stuff!

Then I remembered 1 Corinthians 9:25 where Paul said, "Everyone who competes in the games goes into strict training. They do it to get a crown that will not last; but we do it to get a crown that will last forever." Paul was saying, in effect, "They're all fired up about the wrong race! I would rather that all of you believers trained and practiced and set your sights on winning the *real* race: the one that makes your life count for eternity by the way you serve God and the way you serve people."

Only a few of us will actually be asked to leave our nets and abandon our professions. Not many of us will be led by God to make ministry our career. The vast majority of Christians will be asked to function within their present occupations, but with a whole new mindset, one that reflects God's perspective on the eternal importance of people.

Like me, I'll bet you're thankful that the disciples chose to major in the people business rather than the fishing business. And I'll bet you're glad that in John 21, when Peter considered going back to catching fish, Jesus went to him and renewed his challenge to stay preoccupied with helping people. Three times he told Peter, "Stay with the people business."

That's what Peter did, and he was used by God to impact the entire world. In a much more modest way, that's also what I did, and I'm attempting to have an impact on my corner of the world. The question is, what will *you* do? Where will you invest your life?

Let me implore you, for your own benefit and for the sake of your lost friends, if you love God with all your heart, soul, mind, and strength: *stick to the people business.* Say to the Holy Spirit each day, "Today, let me do more than merely catch fish. Help me do more than just sell a product. Inspire me to go beyond providing a service. Enable me to touch a human life. Work through me to reach a man or a woman for You. I want to be in the people business!" *This* is the mind-set of a contagious Christian.